COOL SPORTS

Skiing

Aaron Carr

MEDIA ENHANCED BOOKS

AV²
BY WEIGL™

ADDED VALUE • AUDIO VISUAL

www.av2books.com

LET'S READ
AV²
BY WEIGL™
ADDED VALUE • AUDIO VISUAL

Go to **www.av2books.com,**
and enter this book's
unique code.

BOOK CODE

K 3 3 3 8 0 2

AV² by Weigl brings you media
enhanced books that support
active learning.

AV² provides enriched content that supplements and complements this book. Weigl's AV² books strive to create inspired learning and engage young minds in a total learning experience.

Your AV² Media Enhanced books come alive with...

Audio
Listen to sections of
the book read aloud.

Video
Watch informative
video clips.

Embedded Weblinks
Gain additional information
for research.

Try This!
Complete activities and
hands-on experiments.

Key Words
Study vocabulary, and
complete a matching
word activity.

Quizzes
Test your knowledge.

Slide Show
View images and
captions, and prepare
a presentation.

... and much, much more!

Published by AV² by Weigl
350 5th Avenue, 59th Floor, New York, NY 10118
Website: www.av2books.com   www.weigl.com

Library of Congress Cataloguing in Publication data available upon request.
Fax 1-866-449-3445 for the attention of the Publishing Records department.

ISBN 978-1-61913-514-7 (hard cover)
ISBN 978-1-61913-520-8 (soft cover)

Printed in the United States of America in North Mankato, Minnesota
1 2 3 4 5 6 7 8 9 16 15 14 13 12

042012
WEP050412

Editor: Aaron Carr   Art Director: Terry Paulhus
Weigl acknowledges Getty Images as the primary image supplier for this title.

2

COOL SPORTS

Skiing

CONTENTS

3

4

Skiing is a winter sport. Some people wear skis to race down hills. Others use skis to do jumps and tricks.

Skis are long thin boards that attach to each foot. They are wider at the ends than in the middle. This helps make turning easier.

Like a PRO

Pro skiers go
very fast on
their skis.

Skiers should always wear a helmet. Helmets keep skiers safe when they fall.

Like a PRO

Pro skiers wear helmets, goggles, gloves, and boots.

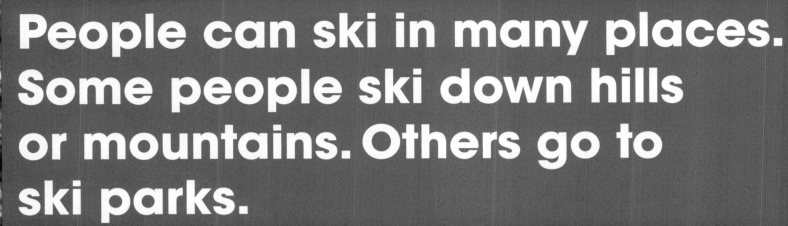

People can ski in many places. Some people ski down hills or mountains. Others go to ski parks.

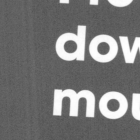

Like a PRO

Pro skiers ski down steep mountains.

It is important for skiers to practice often. This helps them become good skiers.

Like a PRO

Pro skiers practice for many hours every day.

Skiers go off a large ramp and do tricks. This is called Big Air.

Like a PRO

Pro skiers get points for doing hard tricks in Big Air.

15

Skiers ski in a U-shaped ramp and do tricks. This is called Superpipe.

16

Like a PRO

Pro skiers must land many tricks in Superpipe.

Skiers race down a hill with turns and jumps. This is called Skier X.

Like a PRO

Pro skiers race down the hill as fast as they can.

19

Great skiers from all around the world take part in the X Games.

People come to watch the skiers do big jumps and tricks.

21

SKIING FACTS

These pages provide detailed information that expands on the interesting facts found in this book. These pages are intended to be used by adults as a learning support to help young readers round out their knowledge of each sport in the *Cool Sports* series.

Pages 4–5

Skiing is a sport that requires strength and balance. People have been skiing for thousands of years. The oldest skis ever found were more than 7,000 years old. Today, there are many kinds of skiing. The two main types are Nordic and Alpine. Nordic skiing is done on flat trails. Alpine skiing is often called downhill skiing. It is usually done on hills and mountains.

Pages 6–7

Skis used to be made of wood, but today most skis are made of fiberglass and aluminum. Each ski curves inward slightly in the middle. This helps skiers make turns more easily. Some skis bend upward at the front and back. These skis are usually used for doing jumps as they allow the skier to land backwards or forwards. This style of ski is called a twin-tip.

Pages 8–9

The helmet is the most important piece of safety equipment for skiers. If skiers fall and hit their heads without a helmet, they can be seriously injured. Goggles are also important. They protect a skier's eyes from sunlight, snow, and wind. Skiers must also be sure to wear warm, water-resistant clothing. Many skiers wear thermal shirts and pants under a well-insulated ski jacket and snow pants.

Pages 10–11

Skiing can be done anywhere there is a snow-covered hill. Most skiing takes place at ski hills or resorts in mountain ranges. The difficulty of each ski run is marked by colored shapes. A green dot represents the easiest runs, a blue square marks an intermediate run, and a black diamond indicates a difficult run. Expert runs are marked with a double black diamond.

Practice is the most important part of becoming good at any sport, including skiing. Most professional skiers spend the winter practicing their moves on ski hills and in ski parks. They practice their moves in different types of snow, weather, and terrain. Some skiers even try to create new tricks that no other people have seen before.

Big Air began as a snowboarding event at the X Games, but in 1999 it was changed to include skiers. Big Air features four of the world's top skiers trying to outdo each other by completing the best trick. Skiers launch off a large ramp and perform aerial stunts as they soar through the air. Skiers get two attempts to perform their best trick. Tricks are judged for their difficulty.

Superpipe features a 500-foot (152-meter) long, 17-foot (5-m) deep, U-shaped pipe. The pipe is 54 feet (16-m) from edge to edge. The huge pipe allows skiers to gain speed and air so that they can perform tricks. As skiers ride down the slope, they go side to side up the edges of the pipe to launch into the air and complete aerial tricks. More difficult tricks score more points.

Skier X, or Skiercross, is a 3,500-foot (1,067-m) long obstacle course race that features turns, jumps, and gaps. It is a challenging course. The skier that finishes the race with the fastest time wins. Six skiers race each other several times to determine the top skiers. Then, the top skiers race each other one final time. The skier who finishes the final race first wins the gold medal.

The Winter X Games is an annual sports tournament that showcases the best athletes in the extreme sports world. The Winter X Games started in 1997. It includes events for snowboarding, skiing, and snowmobiling. Some of the best skiers in the world compete in the Winter X Games. Some events feature skiers flying through the air or racing down steep hills at high speeds.

KEY WORDS

Research has shown that as much as 65 percent of all written material published in English is made up of 300 words. These 300 words cannot be taught using pictures or learned by sounding them out. They must be recognized by sight. This book contains 63 common sight words to help young readers improve their reading fluency and comprehension. This book also teaches young readers several important content words. These words are paired with pictures to aid in learning and improve understanding.

Page	Sight Words First Appearance
4	a, and, do, down, is, others, people, some, to, use
6	are, at, each, ends, helps, in, long, make, than, that, the, they, this
7	go, like, on, their, very
8	always, keep, should, when
10	can, many, mountains, or, places
12	for, good, important, it, often, them
13	day, every
14	large, off
15	get, hard, points
17	land, must
18	with
19	as
21	all, around, come, from, great, part, take, watch, world

Page	Content Words First Appearance
4	hills, jumps, skiing, skis, sport, tricks
6	boards, foot, middle
7	pro, skiers
8	helmet
9	boots, gloves, goggles
10	ski parks
13	hours
14	Big Air, ramp
16	Superpipe
18	Skier X, turns
21	X Games

Check out av2books.com for activities, videos, audio clips, and more!

1 Go to av2books.com

2 Enter book code   K 3 3 3 8 0 2

3 Fuel your imagination online!

24

www.av2books.com